TRICKSTERS
from
Around the World

by Lesli Favor

illustrated by Dwight Francis

Table of Contents

What Is a TRICKSTER?

Tricksters are a type of **character** in stories. Tricksters love to play tricks on other characters. They are clever, but they can be greedy and prideful, too. Often they act before they think. A trickster's trick might get him into trouble or make him look silly.

▲ Anansi is a spider who plays tricks on his friends.

A good example is the hare in the story of the hare and the tortoise. The hare challenges the tortoise to a race. The race is a trick. The hare knows that he is much faster than the tortoise. He will have no trouble winning the race.

However, the hare is prideful. He is so sure that he will win that he lies down to take a nap during the race. While he sleeps, the tortoise wins the race. In the end, the hare looks silly.

People all around the world have stories about tricksters. Different countries and cultures have their own favorite tricksters. Some of them are animals and others are fairies. All of them talk and act like people.

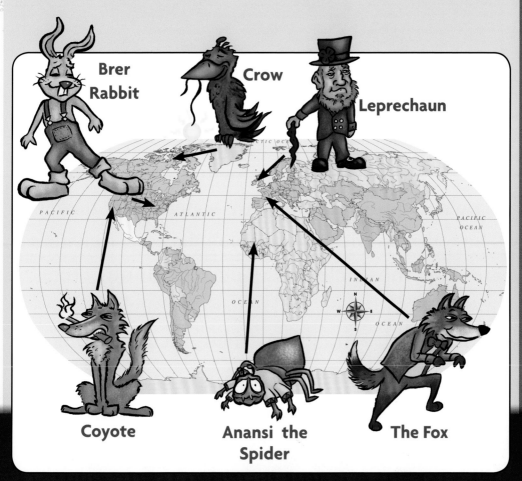

What Are Some Different TRICKSTERS?

Have you ever seen a clown trick someone? Clowns squirt people with water from flowers. They throw pies in people's faces. Tricksters are like those clowns. They are funny, they are silly, and they make people laugh. Some tricksters play tricks on their friends. Others trick gods to help humans.

Brer Rabbit is a trickster from the United States. In one story, Brer Rabbit is bored and wants to have some fun. He leads his friends to the pond. It is night, and the water is like a mirror. It looks like the moon is lying on top of the water.

▲ The story of Brer Rabbit and the moon is one of many tales about this trickster. *Brer* means "brother."

Brer Rabbit tricks his friends into thinking that the moon has fallen into the pond. His friends dive in to save the moon. They are soaked, but they can't catch the moon. Brer Rabbit stands on dry land and laughs. He isn't bored anymore!

Brer Rabbit in Literature

Stories about Brer Rabbit were collected in this book by Joel Chandler Harris. It was published in 1881. Many other people have written down their versions of the Brer Rabbit tales.

NATIVE AMERICAN

Native Americans tell tales about Coyote. He tricks the fire gods into sharing fire with humans. First, Coyote steals a burning stick from the fire gods. As they chase him, he passes the fire to Cougar. Cougar passes the fire to Fox, and so on, from animal to animal.

The last animal puts the fire into a piece of wood. The gods cannot get the fire out of the wood. They have been tricked! This was Coyote's plan all along. Coyote shows humans how to get fire out of wood, and this is how people first got fire.

Crow is a trickster who steals daylight. The north part of the world is always dark, but the south part has daylight. Crow tricks people in the south so he can steal a ball of daylight. He takes the daylight to the north. After that, the north has daylight, too.

▲ Crow is another Native American trickster.

In West Africa, people tell stories about Anansi the spider. In one Anansi tale, Turtle comes for dinner at Anansi's house. But Anansi is greedy. He doesn't want to share his yummy yams. He tricks Turtle into leaving the house. While Turtle is gone, Anansi eats all the yams.

▲ Anansi tells Turtle he must go wash his hands. But he knows Turtle's hands will get dirty again when he walks back to the house, again and again.

Another day, Turtle fixes lunch for Anansi at the bottom of the pond. Anansi loads his coat with rocks so he can sink down. But Turtle asks Anansi to take off his coat. When Anansi does, he floats to the top of the water. Now Anansi has no coat and no lunch!

▲ Turtle knew that Anansi had tricked him, so he tricked Anansi back!

IRELAND

In Irish folktales, leprechauns hide pots of gold. A person who looks into a leprechaun's eyes can ask him where his gold is hidden. The leprechaun must answer truthfully. However, the leprechaun might offer to grant three wishes instead. Usually, the person's wishes backfire.

EUROPE

The fox is a trickster in tales all across Europe. The French call him Reynard the Fox. He is always clever and sly.

Real-Life Tricksters

Think about the tricksters in this book. They are animals, but they are helpful, prideful, greedy, clever, sly, and silly, the way people can be. Have you ever seen a real animal behave like any of these tricksters? What did the animal do?

Reynard the Fox wants the honey that belongs to Bruin the Bear. Reynard pretends to go visit friends, but he sneaks back and eats his friend's honey. Bruin the Bear notices that the honey is gone. Then Reynard tricks him into thinking he ate it himself.

Why Do Stories Have **TRICKSTERS**?

Tricksters make us laugh, but they also teach us lessons or **morals**. When the hare loses the race with the tortoise, it is funny. But it also teaches a lesson. Slow and steady wins the race.

When Turtle tricks Anansi out of lunch, it is funny. Anansi had done the same thing to Turtle! But the story also teaches that being greedy doesn't pay. Is it a good idea to have your wishes come true? Stories about leprechauns often teach us to be "careful what we wish for."

Some trickster stories try to answer questions about our world. How did people first discover fire? Why does the spider have no coat? Why are there rainbows? Trickster stories from around the world give fun answers to questions like these.

Glossary

character (KAIR-ik-ter): a person or animal that is part of a story (page 2)

moral (MOR-ul): a rule of behavior that tells right from wrong (page 17)

trickster (TRIK-ster): a person or animal who plays tricks on others (page 2)

Index